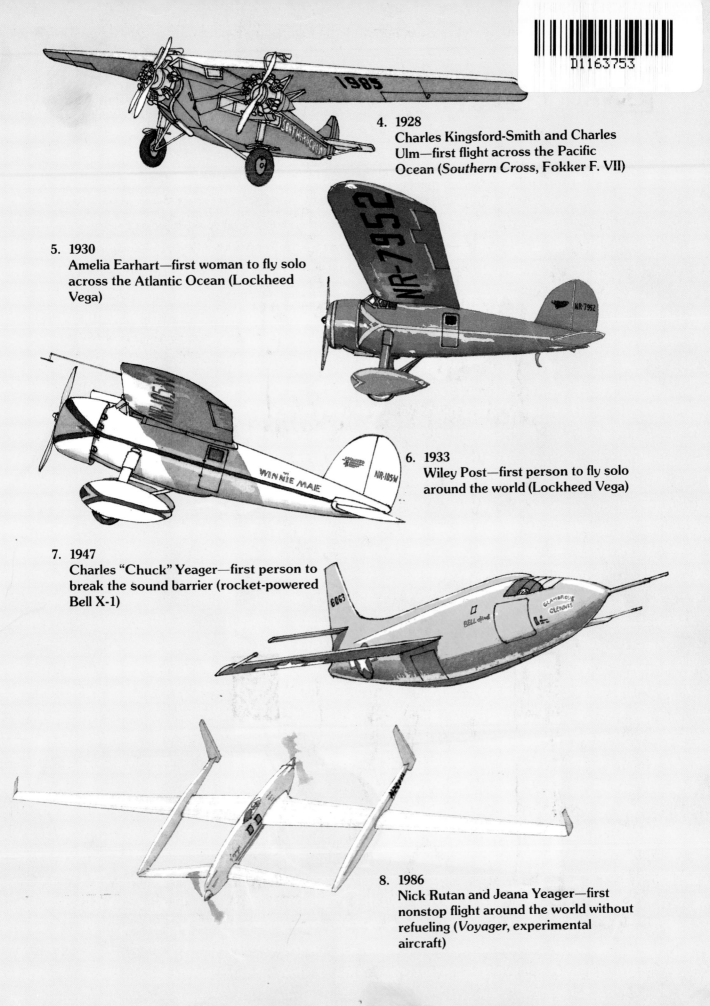

4. 1928
Charles Kingsford-Smith and Charles Ulm—first flight across the Pacific Ocean (*Southern Cross*, Fokker F. VII)

5. 1930
Amelia Earhart—first woman to fly solo across the Atlantic Ocean (Lockheed Vega)

6. 1933
Wiley Post—first person to fly solo around the world (Lockheed Vega)

7. 1947
Charles "Chuck" Yeager—first person to break the sound barrier (rocket-powered Bell X-1)

8. 1986
Nick Rutan and Jeana Yeager—first nonstop flight around the world without refueling (*Voyager*, experimental aircraft)

For Earl — G.I.

For my late father, George; my mother, Rose; my wife, Rita;
my children, Lisa, Beth, George III, and Christopher; and
our late, dear friend and teacher, Philip Hicken — G.G.

Special thanks to: Dana Bell, National Air & Space Museum; the Boeing Company; Col. Frederick J. Christensen, Jr., US Air Force, Ret.; Evan Hull, Massport; Jane Monahan, The Port Authority of New York & New Jersey; Alice Price, Public Affairs, Office of the Secretary of the Air Force; Robert Schulman, Chief, Special Services Branch, National Aeronautics and Space Administration; Maj. Peter Vergados, US Air Force, Ret.; and Ann Whyte, Pan Am.

THE BIG BOOK OF REAL
AIRPLANES

By Gina Ingoglia

Illustrated by George Guzzi

Grosset & Dunlap · New York

Airplanes have existed for less than 100 years. Before that time, people simply wished that they could fly. Some of them even strapped big wings on their backs, hoping for success. But no matter how hard they flapped, *no one* ever took off! Here are some early flying machines that helped us get off the ground.

About the year 1500, Leonardo da Vinci, an Italian artist and inventor, drew plans for a flying machine with moving wings. It was called an ornithopter. But it was only a drawing. No one ever built one.

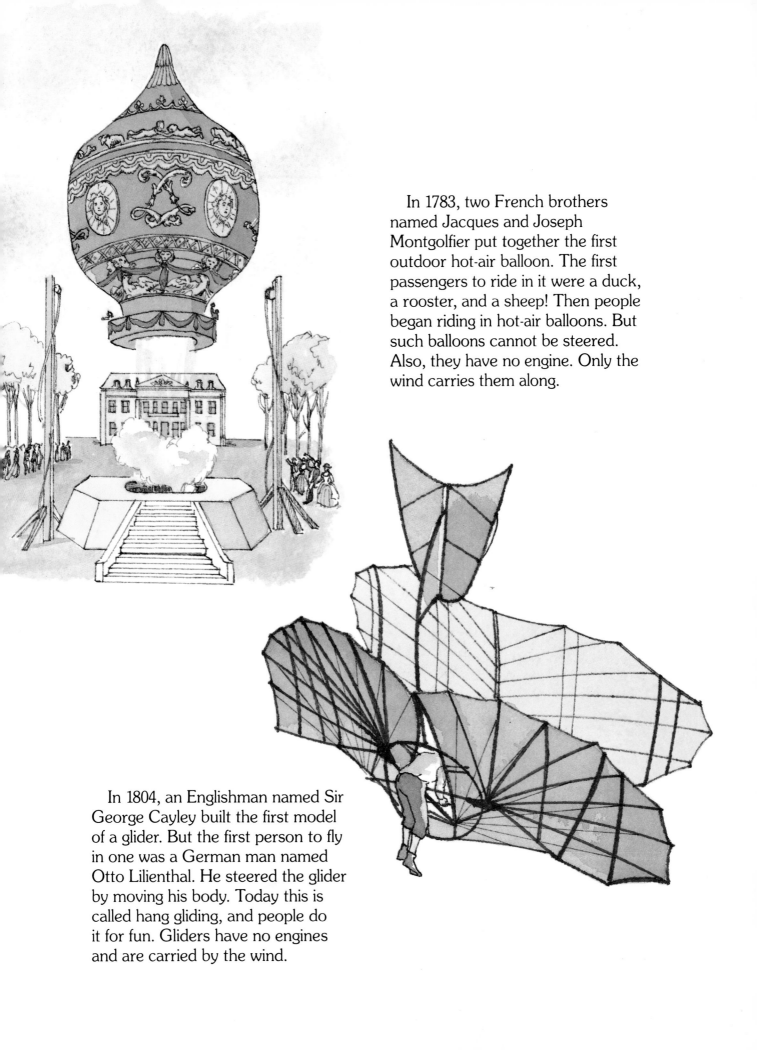

In 1783, two French brothers named Jacques and Joseph Montgolfier put together the first outdoor hot-air balloon. The first passengers to ride in it were a duck, a rooster, and a sheep! Then people began riding in hot-air balloons. But such balloons cannot be steered. Also, they have no engine. Only the wind carries them along.

In 1804, an Englishman named Sir George Cayley built the first model of a glider. But the first person to fly in one was a German man named Otto Lilienthal. He steered the glider by moving his body. Today this is called hang gliding, and people do it for fun. Gliders have no engines and are carried by the wind.

Two American brothers from Ohio, Wilbur and Orville Wright, performed the first powered flight. The Wright Brothers built bicycles, but they were also particularly interested in kites and gliders. In 1903 they built an aircraft which they named *Flyer I*. It had two very important features—propellers and a gasoline engine—to provide power. The airplane didn't have to be carried by the wind like a glider or a hot-air balloon.

The first flight was near Kill Devil Hill at Kitty Hawk, North Carolina. The flight lasted only twelve seconds and *Flyer I* traveled 120 feet, less than half the length of a football field!

Interest in flying continued to grow and new developments spread rapidly. With the creation of the airplane, the world of aviation would never be the same again.

What Keeps an Airplane Up?

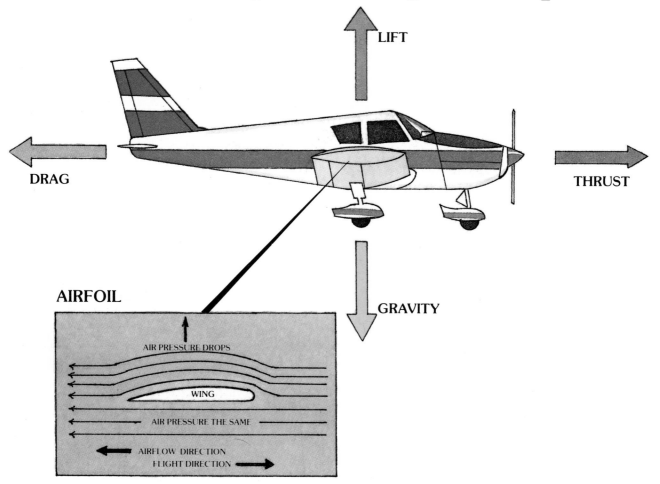

To fly, an airplane must overpower what is called **drag**, the force of air against a plane moving forward. It resists or slows down the plane. The plane's engines create a force of their own called **thrust**, providing power to move forward. When thrust is greater than drag, the plane continues to move forward.

Another force that must be overcome is **gravity**. Gravity is the natural force that keeps things on the ground. (If it weren't for gravity, we'd float around in the air!) A plane is very heavy and the force of gravity holding it down is great. But the plane overcomes gravity through its wing design.

The shape of the wing is quite important. A wing is an example of an airfoil. The top of the wing is curved, and as the plane moves forward, pressure of the air rushing over the curve lessens. The air underneath the wing moves in a straight line, and its pressure is high, or greater than that over the wing. High-pressure air pushes up against the wing to meet the low-pressure air. Result: the plane rises. The wings have created a force called **lift**.

As long as an airplane's forces of lift and thrust are greater than the outside forces of gravity and drag, it is able to take off and fly.

How Aircraft Engines Work

RECIPROCATING ENGINE

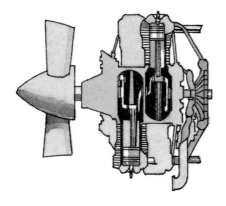

The engine that turns a propeller is called a reciprocating engine. As air moves into the engine, it is squeezed into a very small space. Then it is forced into a cylinder to burn with the fuel. As the air is heated, it takes up more space and pushes against a piston. The moving piston turns a crankshaft attached to the propellers. The turning propellers push air behind them and this makes the plane move forward.

TURBOJET

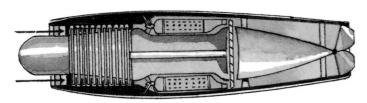

The turbojet is a basic jet engine. As air moves into the front of the engine, it is forced into a very small space by the compressor. The air is heated by fuel in the combustion chamber. Hot air takes up much more space, and it shoots out of an exhaust nozzle at the back of the engine. This strong exhaust force moves backward and causes the plane itself to move forward.

TURBOPROP

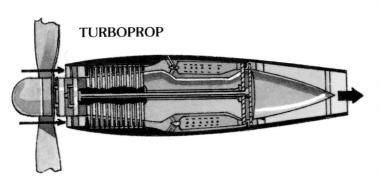

The turboprop was designed to save fuel. The turboprop uses turbojet engines to turn propellers. The propellers help bring in air to work the engines, so less fuel has to be used. Propellers don't work as well above certain speeds. But the turboprop is very useful at low speeds.

TURBOFAN

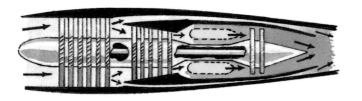

The turbofan has large fans mounted inside the front of a turbojet engine. The fans pull in huge amounts of air and cut down on fuel needed to form the jet exhaust. Turbofans can work well at speeds over 400 miles an hour.

How to Fly a Plane

Planes have three movements called **pitch**, **roll**, and **yaw**. A plane pitches when its nose moves up or down. When one wing is tipped higher or lower than the other, the plane is rolling. A plane yaws when its nose is turned to the left or right. The pilot is able to control pitch, roll, and yaw by moving parts of the plane's wings and tail.

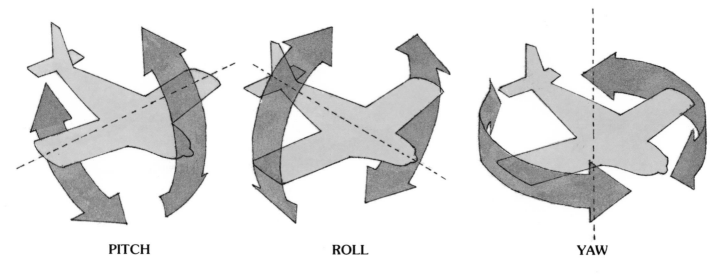

PITCH   **ROLL**   **YAW**

To steer the plane to the right or left and control the roll movement, the pilot moves the **ailerons**, small flaps on the back edge of each wing. The pilot controls them with the control wheel. When the control wheel or stick is moved to the right, the aileron on the right wing goes up and the left aileron goes down. Air moves more slowly across the right wing and air pressure on that wing builds up. This causes the right wing to dip down. The plane banks, or turns, to the right. When the stick is moved to the left, the left aileron goes up and the right one goes down. Now the plane banks to the left.

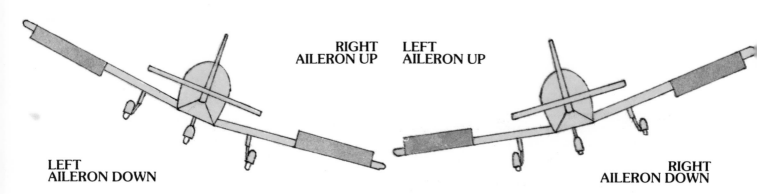

RIGHT AILERON UP   **LEFT AILERON UP**

LEFT AILERON DOWN   **RIGHT AILERON DOWN**

A plane turns left or right by means of the **rudder**. This controls the yaw movement. The rudder is on the back of the tail and the pilot controls its back-and-forth movement with two foot pedals. When the right pedal is pushed, the rudder moves to the right. The wind blowing against it pushes the tail to the left. This makes the plane's nose point to the right so the plane flies to the right. In the same way, the left pedal makes the plane's nose point to the left.

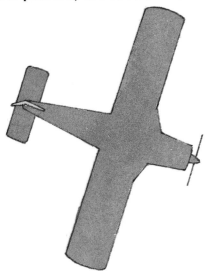

RUDDER TURNED TO RIGHT

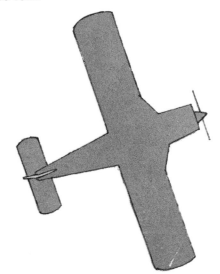

RUDDER TURNED TO LEFT

The **elevators**, also on the tail, cause the nose to point up or down. They control the pitch movement. The pilot controls the elevators by moving the control wheel or stick forward or backward. When it is pushed forward, the elevators move down. The air blowing against them pushes the tail up, and the nose of the plane points down. When the stick is pulled back, the elevators go up. The air blowing against them pushes the tail down, and the plane begins to climb.

ELEVATOR DOWN

ELEVATOR UP

Another way to make planes point up or down is with the **throttle**, located in the cockpit. The throttle controls the engine and the propellers. When the throttle is pushed in, the engine goes faster and the plane begins to climb. When the throttle is pulled out, the engine slows down and the plane starts to point down.

The **Boeing Model 314** was a famous flying boat. During the 1920s and 1930s many people used it to fly across the ocean. This unusual aircraft used water surfaces, instead of the ground, for takeoffs and landings. Flying boats looked as if they were half plane and half boat. The top part had wings and the bottom part had a hull or boat body.

The Boeing Model 314 weighed 42 tons. It flew the first regular passenger service across the Atlantic Ocean. This service began on July 8, 1939, and ended during World War II.

Other famous flying boats were the China Clipper, which flew across the Pacific Ocean, and the Dornier Do-X from Germany. The Dornier Do-X was a huge flying boat that carried almost 170 passengers and had twelve engines paired back to back.

Propeller Planes

▶ The **Douglas DC-3** is a large passenger plane, or airliner. The DC-3 was first flown in 1935 and held 21 passengers. It was the first popular airliner used worldwide. Many are still used today.

▼ A **crop duster** dusts crops with chemicals that keep away harmful insects and plant diseases. Flying a crop duster can be very dangerous. It must be flown low, often quite close to trees and high-tension wires.

◄The **Canadair CL-215** is called a "flying boat." It is also a water bomber. It scoops up water from lakes and rivers at 81 miles per hour and dumps it on top of forest fires. It takes only 10 seconds to fill up with 1,386 gallons of water!

▼ The **Piper Cub Cheyenne III** is used for "hops" or short trips. The first was built in 1931. These small "light" planes are very popular. Because they are so easy to fly, thousands have been built for personal and commercial use.

A **helicopter** is a type of aircraft that can take off and land in a small space. It doesn't need a runway because it rises straight up in the air. This is called a vertical takeoff.

A helicopter has no wings. Instead, it has a rotor on the top that looks like a large propeller. The rotor consists of blades that spin around very fast. As the blades spin, the air on top *pulls* the blade up, and the air below *pushes* it up. This pulling and pushing of air against the blades causes the helicopter to rise.

The pilot can tilt the rotor blades and move the helicopter in all directions. A helicopter usually has a smaller rotor on its tail. If it didn't, the whole helicopter would spin round and round. The small rotor also helps the pilot to steer. Some helicopters have two large rotors on top that turn in opposite directions. This also prevents the helicopter from spinning around.

Helicopters are called "choppers" or "whirlybirds." They are slower than airplanes and harder to fly. The pilot has to control the direction of the helicopter as well as the tilt of the blades.

"Choppers" at Work

Helicopters are able to do four things that make them very useful:

▶ **They need very little room to take off and land.** This makes them very important during wartime for moving troops and supplies out of tight places.

▼ **They can hover.** This means that they can "hang" in the air without moving. A hovering helicopter can rescue people at sea or from a burning building.

◄ **They can fly slowly.** Radio and television reporters have time to study road conditions and inform motorists about traffic tie-ups.

▼ **They can pick up great weight.** The Sikorsky S-64 Skycrane is used by the U.S. Army to move large equipment. It can even pick up small buildings!

Jet Planes

Jet engines make it possible for planes to travel long distances at high speeds.

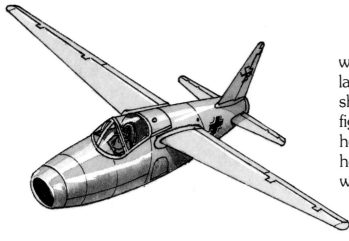

The **Heinkel He 178** made the world's very first jet flight. Like its later version, the He 162 Salamander shown here, it was a German fighter warplane. Germans had hoped that the Heinkel He would help them win World War II. But it was built too late to be of much use.

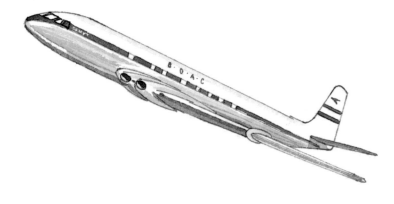

The **de Havilland Comet 1** was the first jet airliner. It was produced in Great Britain and first flew in 1949. Because of structural flaws, the Comet 1 was replaced by the Comet 4, shown here. It first flew across the Atlantic Ocean in April 1958.

The **Boeing 707** was the first jet airliner produced in the United States. In 1958 it began jet service between New York and Paris. The early 707s carried 130 passengers. But these jets were so popular that they were redesigned to carry 189 people.

These popular jet airliners look very similar.
Each plane has three engines, but they are arranged differently.

The **Boeing 727** carries from 94 to 189 passengers and flies at 542 to 592 miles per hour. All of its engines are at the rear of the plane. The center one is inside the tail fin, buried in the fuselage (the body of the plane).

The **McDonnell Douglas DC-10** carries from 255 to 380 passengers and flies at 540 to 594 miles per hour. It has one engine under each wing. The center engine is on the outside of the tail, not inside the fuselage.

The **Lockheed Tristar L-1011** carries from 256 to 400 passengers and flies at 553 to 605 miles per hour. It has one engine under each wing, like the DC-10, but the center engine is buried in the fuselage, as in the 727.

How Big Is a Jumbo Jet?

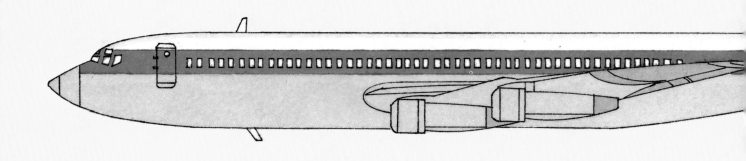

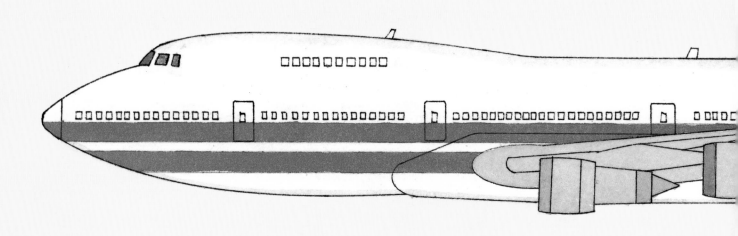

length of Wright Brothers' first flight:
120 feet

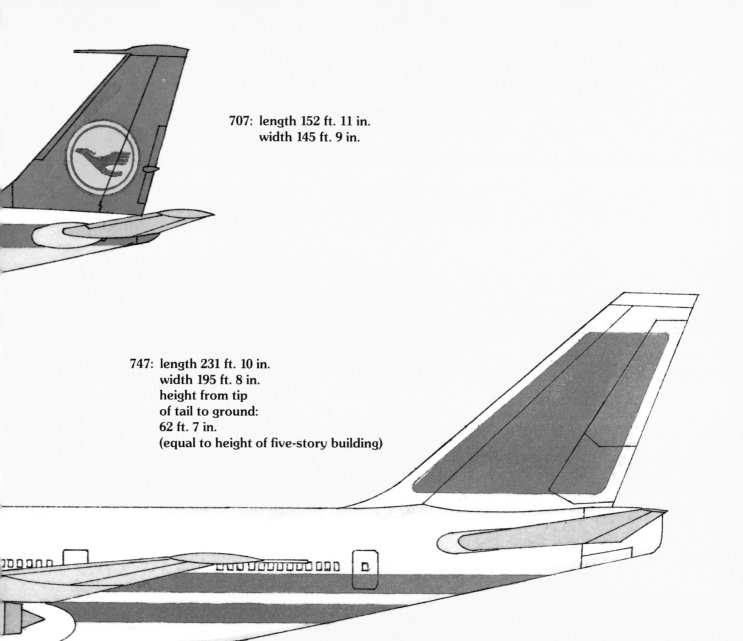

707: length 152 ft. 11 in.
width 145 ft. 9 in.

747: length 231 ft. 10 in.
width 195 ft. 8 in.
height from tip
of tail to ground:
62 ft. 7 in.
(equal to height of five-story building)

The Boeing 747 was the first jumbo jet. It began service in 1970. This huge jet can fly 607 miles per hour and carry 500 passengers. The 747 weighs 800,000 pounds, about the same as 250 cars! But it needs no more runway length than the smaller 707 because of the 747's powerful, specially-designed engines. Newer engines make it possible for a 747 to fly from New York to Tokyo, Japan, without stopping to refuel.

Boeing 747 Jumbo Jet

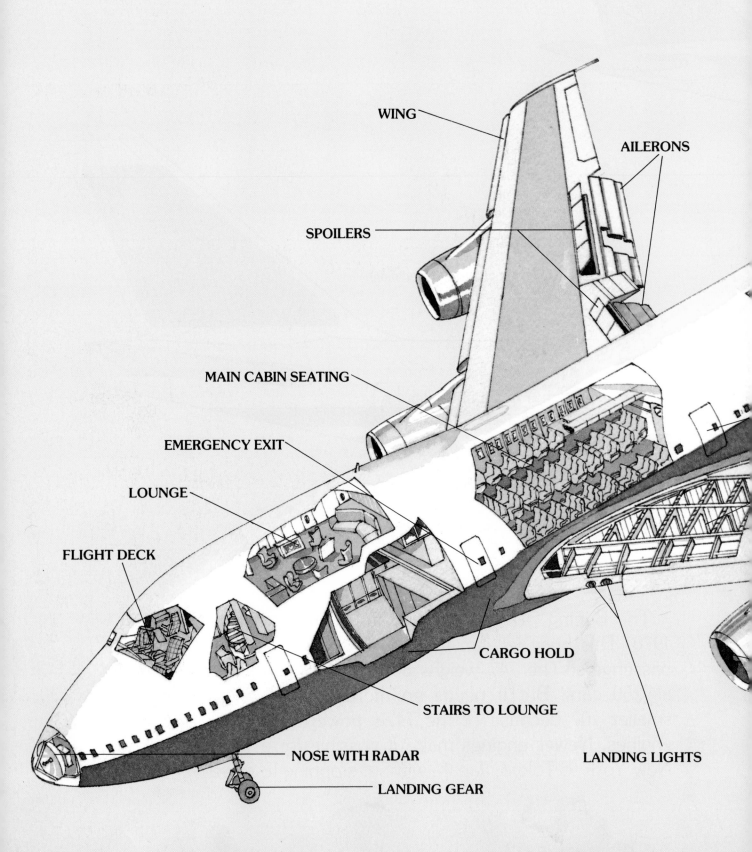

WING

AILERONS

SPOILERS

MAIN CABIN SEATING

EMERGENCY EXIT

LOUNGE

FLIGHT DECK

CARGO HOLD

STAIRS TO LOUNGE

NOSE WITH RADAR

LANDING LIGHTS

LANDING GEAR

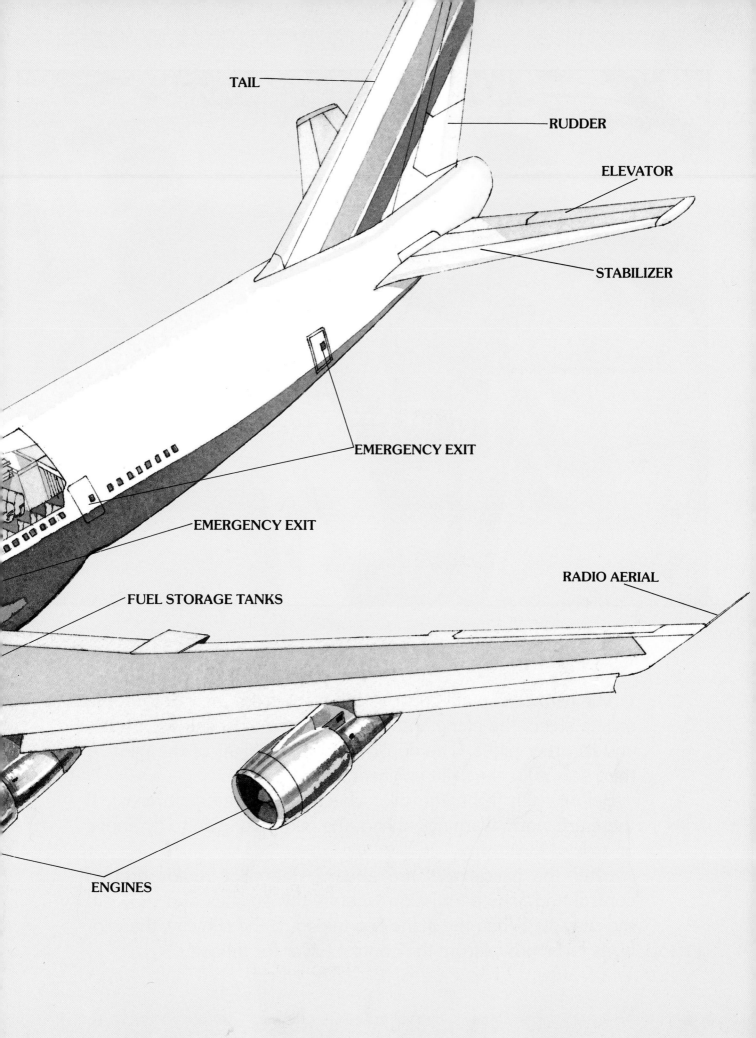

TAIL

RUDDER

ELEVATOR

STABILIZER

EMERGENCY EXIT

EMERGENCY EXIT

RADIO AERIAL

FUEL STORAGE TANKS

ENGINES

The pilot or captain controls the plane from the **cockpit**. He or she steers the plane and uses the radio to speak to airports and to other pilots. The copilot sits to the right of the pilot. A third seat is for the flight engineer.

Before each flight, the pilot checks the weather forecast. If there are storm warnings ahead, the pilot may plan to fly above or around the storm.

After the passengers are aboard, the pilot radios ground control and asks permission to start the engines and move to the runway. When the plane has taxied to the runway, the pilot waits for approval from the control tower for takeoff.

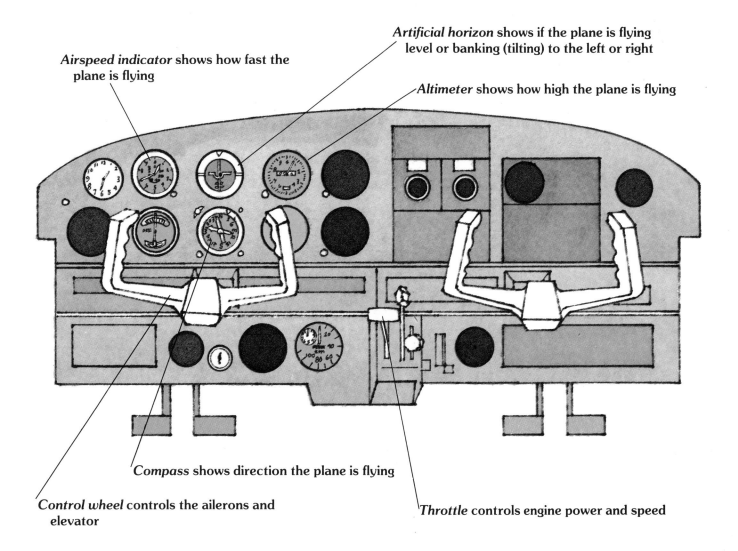

Artificial horizon shows if the plane is flying level or banking (tilting) to the left or right

Airspeed indicator shows how fast the plane is flying

Altimeter shows how high the plane is flying

Compass shows direction the plane is flying

Control wheel controls the ailerons and elevator

Throttle controls engine power and speed

Cockpit instruments are very important. Without them the pilot wouldn't know how fast, how high, or what direction the plane was flying. Instruments also indicate how the engines are running. When it is time to land, the automatic landing system takes over and lands the plane. Most planes built today have automatic landing systems.

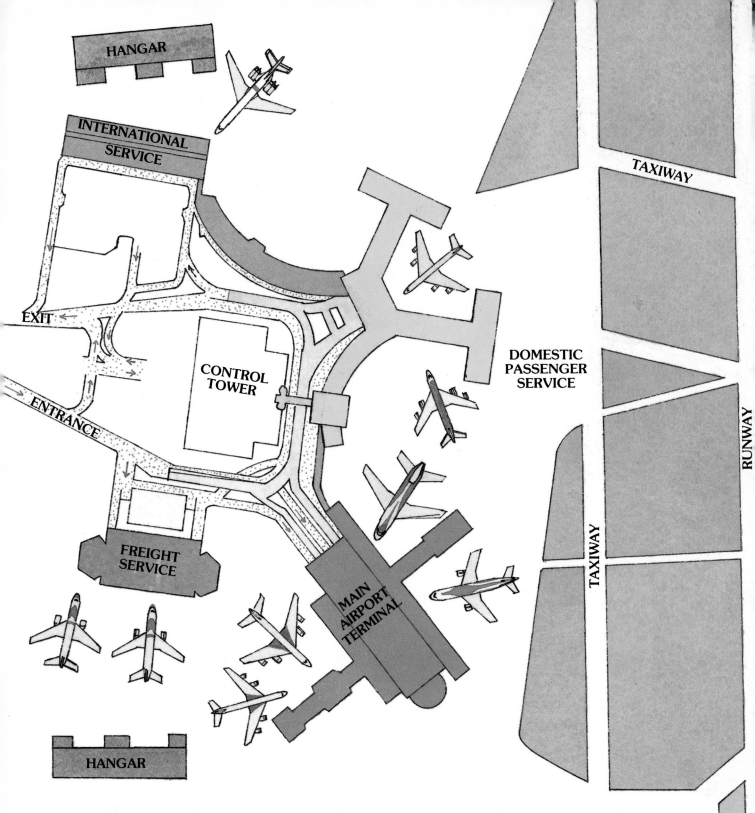

Airports take up plenty of room. From the air they look like long, wide roads crossing one another. These roads are the runways. Planes need very long runways for takeoffs and landings. The shorter roads leading to the runways are called taxiways. At night the runways and taxiways are outlined with lights so that pilots can see them easily.

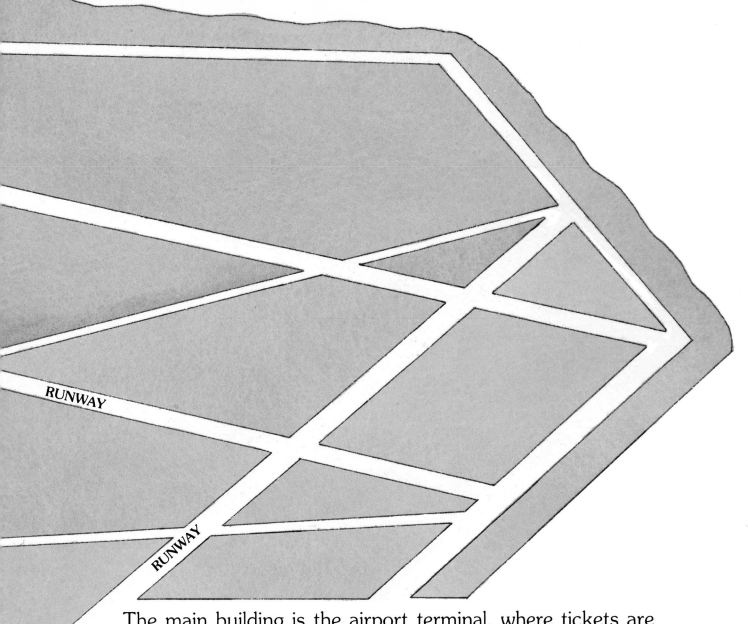

RUNWAY

RUNWAY

The main building is the airport terminal, where tickets are sold and where people meet incoming and outgoing flights. Incoming planes are called arrivals. Outgoing planes are called departures. Terminals in large airports may have restaurants and shops.

Other large buildings at an airport are the hangars. Planes are repaired in hangars and made safe and ready for future flights.

A very important airport building is the control tower. Air traffic controllers keep track of all planes that are flying in or near the airport. The planes are watched on radar screens, where they look like small, moving dots of light, called blips.

From high in the air, airports look as if there isn't much going on. But on the ground there are many people working at many different jobs.

Who's Who at the Airport

Here are some people who work hard
to make air travel safe, easy, and enjoyable.

Cabin crew includes the pilot, co-pilot, and flight engineer.

Flight attendants look after the safety and comfort of passengers and serve meals.

Airplane mechanics and **maintenance technicians** check the plane's engines and mechanical parts and refuel the plane before every flight. No plane is allowed to take off until these people say it is ready to fly.

Catering staffs take care of planning and preparing meals for passengers in kitchens on the ground. Imagine how much food is needed to feed 500 people on a jumbo jet!

Aircraft cleaners make sure the planes are scrubbed and neat inside and out.

Air freight and **air mail agents** are responsible for seeing that tons of mail and freight sent by air move quickly and safely.

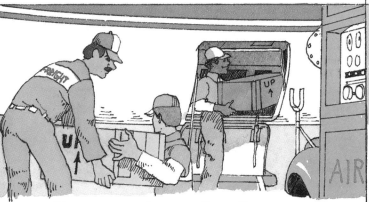

Baggage and **cargo handlers** load and unload everything that travels in the holds of the planes.

Tower control personnel (air traffic controllers) talk back and forth to pilots, telling them when to take off and land, and which runways to use.

Airline and **airport security people** are constantly looking for ways to keep anything or anyone dangerous away from the airport, the airplanes, and the passengers.

Airport maintenance crews keep the runways and roads in good condition.

A Trip on an Airplane

Lissy and John have arrived at the airport to take their first plane trip. Here are some of the things they see and do.

1. The first stop is the check-in counter, to buy tickets, choose plane seats, and check in luggage.

2. Then Lissy and John go to the departure gate. But first they pass through a security check. Everything is X-rayed to make sure nothing dangerous goes inside the plane.

3. On board the plane Lissy puts her carry-on bag under the seat. As soon as Lissy and John sit down, they fasten their seat belts.

4. As the plane taxis to the runway, a flight attendant explains the plane's safety equipment and tells where the emergency exits are located.

5. The plane speeds down the runway and lifts off the ground. As Lissy and John look down, the airport buildings seem smaller and smaller.

6. In a few minutes, the plane is above the clouds. "They look like fluffy pillows," says John.

7. At lunchtime the flight attendant wheels the food cart down the aisle. Lissy and John use the little "tables" that flip down from the seats in front of them to hold their trays.

8. After lunch Lissy reads a magazine and listens to music from a headset. John watches a movie. He hears the sound through a special channel on his headset.

9. When it's time to land, the seat belt sign lights up. As the plane descends, John's and Lissy's ears feel funny. "If you swallow, it helps," says Lissy.

10. In the airport, Lissy and John meet their aunt and uncle. Then they go to the baggage-claim area to pick up their suitcases. "Our flight was super," John says. "Airplanes are lots of fun."

The **Concorde** is a supersonic transport (SST) plane that was built by the French and British governments. *Supersonic* means that this plane travels faster than the speed of sound.

The Concorde's first flight was in 1969. This plane carries 100 passengers and flies at Mach 2 (twice the speed of sound). At 1,335 miles per hour, the Concorde flies faster than a speeding bullet! The Concorde is 204 feet long, but during supersonic flight the outside forces and heat are so great that the plane stretches about 10 inches! But this isn't a problem. The Concorde's special aluminum-alloy body is made to hold up under this change.

When a plane flies at supersonic speeds, the air in front of it becomes very hard because the air doesn't have time to move away. The wall of air is called the "sound barrier." When the plane hits the barrier, a shock wave is formed, causing a very loud sound called a "sonic boom." Hitting the sound barrier would destroy regular planes, but the Concorde is shaped to "cut" its way through the air with its long needle nose and very thin delta (swept-back) wings. During landing, the nose is lowered to droop so the pilot can see better.

The **SR 71A "Blackbird"** is a famous reconnaissance plane. Reconnaissance or search planes are military craft that keep track of what's going on in enemy lands. They fly very high and very fast without being seen.

The Blackbird has a two-man crew and flies at Mach 3, or 2,185 miles per hour (three times the speed of sound). When planes fly faster than Mach 2.2, their outer surface gets so hot that it has to be made out of special material that can stand great heat. This heat is caused by the friction of the plane's surface moving against the air around it.

The Blackbird has equipment that can make special maps of 60,000 square miles of the earth's surface in just one hour. Also on board are cameras so powerful that they can focus on something as small as a golf ball on the ground. That is amazing, because the Blackbird flies 15 miles high. (Imagine the height of 65 Empire State Buildings stacked one on top of another!)

The **Hawker Siddeley Harrier** is a vertical takeoff and landing (VTOL) combat aircraft from Great Britain. A VTOL looks like an ordinary plane, but it takes off and lands like a helicopter. It can also hover and fly backward. It has special jet engines with four nozzles that the pilot controls from the cockpit. When the nozzles are pointed downward, the plane moves straight up or down. When the nozzles are pointed backward, the plane flies forward. By moving the nozzles during a "dogfight" (a fight with another plane), the pilot can fly quickly in all directions. VTOL planes are also useful for landing and taking off from small areas without runways or from aircraft carriers (ships that carry airplanes).

The **Boeing E-3 Sentry** is one of the most expensive and important planes ever built. It is usually called AWACS (pronounced "A-Wax"), which stands for Airborne Warning and Control System.

An AWACS flies at 530 miles per hour with a flying crew of four people and thirteen AWACS specialists. It is packed with high-speed computers and carries a large radome on its back, which has powerful antennae inside. AWACS planes can act as flying command posts during wartime by sending information to other aircraft, ships, and military bases on the ground. By working together, AWACS planes have the ability to control the entire United States Air Force if necessary.

The **F-14 Tomcat** was built for the U.S. Navy and is one of the finest warplanes today. It is a swing-wing twin-engined fighter.

A plane with delta (swept-back) wings can move through the air at high speeds. A plane with wings that stick out straight is easier to handle at lower speeds and during takeoffs and landings. A swing-wing plane has both advantages.

The pilot controls the wings from the cockpit and changes them from one shape to the other. When straight wings are needed for takeoffs and landings, the wings are moved forward. When swept-back wings are needed for high-speed flying, the wings are moved back to form a delta wing.

The Tomcat can reach speeds of Mach 2.34, or 1,545 miles per hour (over two times the speed of sound). It carries Phoenix missiles that can hit targets 100 miles away!

Flying has become the quickest way to travel. So much has happened in such a short time that it is hard to tell what might happen next. But one thing is sure—there will always be people designing and testing new and better planes.

◄ The **Space Shuttle** developed by the National Aeronautics and Space Administration (NASA), takes off from a launching pad like traditional spacecraft. To blast off, the shuttle is assisted by recoverable booster rockets and a large fuel tank. During flight, the rockets fall away and the empty fuel tank is dumped. The Shuttle then flies on its own. The unique feature is that the Shuttle lands like a plane. Although the Shuttle is not new, it is constantly studied and tested for improvements.

► The **Grumman X-29** is part of a series of "X" aircraft that are built to test new aeronautic designs. This strange-looking craft was built to study the advantage of forward-swept wings. The shape of the wings makes the plane easier to maneuver or control. This plane has a computer system that allows the pilot to make changes on the outer parts of the plane forty times a second!

The X-29 is 48 feet long, has a crew of one, and can reach a speed of Mach 1.05 (just over the speed of sound). You can identify the front end by the long needle nose.

Aeronautical Terms

aeronautical—having to do with aircraft

aileron—a surface on the rear edge of a wing that moves to make an airplane turn

aircraft—any type of vehicle intended to fly in the atmosphere, including hot-air balloons

airliner—a large passenger plane

airplane—an aircraft with a fixed wing and engine

airport—a place where airplanes take off and land; usually has hangars where airplanes are housed, and buildings for passengers and freight

airspeed indicator—an instrument that measures how fast a plane is flying

altimeter—an instrument that measures how high a plane is flying

artificial horizon—an instrument that shows whether a plane is flying levelly or turning

autopilot—a device that flies a plane automatically

bank—the tilt of a plane to the right or left

cockpit—the space set aside for the pilot and crew on an airplane; if enclosed, called a cabin

control stick—stick used by the pilot to control the ailerons and elevators; also called a yoke or joy stick

drag—a natural force of air that slows down a plane by opposing its movement forward

elevator—a surface on the edge of the tail that moves to make a plane go up or down

fixed wing—a wing that doesn't move or "flap"

flying boat—a kind of seaplane with a body that serves as a boat for landing on water

friction—heat caused by a plane's surface moving against the air around it

fuselage—the body of an airplane, to which the wings and tail are attached

glider—a light, engineless aircraft that floats on air currents

gravity—a natural force that pulls a plane to the ground

hangar—a building or structure that houses a plane

helicopter—an aircraft that takes off and lands straight up and down (vertically)

hop—a short flight

instrument panel—a board on which a plane's instruments are installed

jumbo jet—a very large airliner

landing gear—the underpart of an aircraft, including the wheels, that supports the airplane when it lands

lift—a force that opposes gravity and helps a plane to rise

Mach number—the number indicating the speed of an aircraft as compared to the speed of sound

pilot—the person who flies the aircraft; also called the captain on airliners

pitch—the upward or downward movement of the plane's nose

reciprocating engine—a basic propeller engine

roll—the movement of one wing higher or lower than the other

rotor—spinning "wing" of a helicopter

rudder—hinged part of the tail that steers a plane from one side to another

runway—a strip of ground for plane takeoffs and landings

solo—to fly alone

sonic boom—the sound made when a plane hits the sound barrier

sound barrier—the invisible "wall" of air that planes hit as they approach the speed of sound

taxi—to operate a plane on the ground or on water

throttle—a control that affects the speed of the engine

thrust—a force that opposes drag and makes the plane move forward

turbofan—a jet engine with large, powerful, fuel-saving fans

turbojet—a basic jet engine

turboprop—a jet engine with propellers

twin-engine—having two engines

yaw—the movement of a plane's nose to the left or right

Military Planes

1. **Fokker DVII**
   (Germany 1918)
   Famous World War I fighter

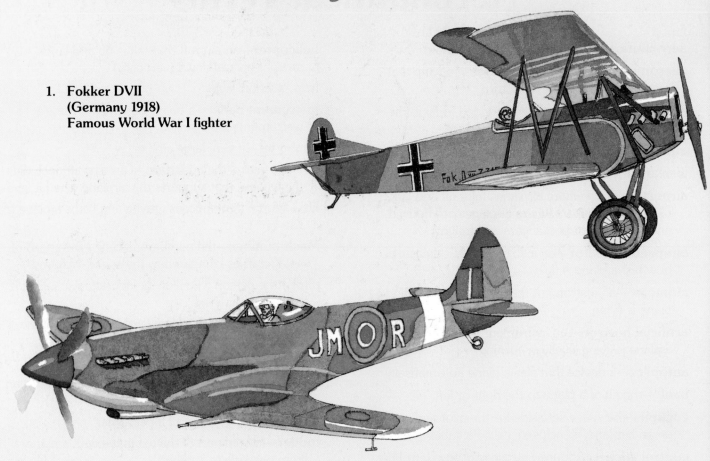

2. **Spitfire**
   (Great Britain 1936)
   Best fighter in the Battle of Britain
   in World War II

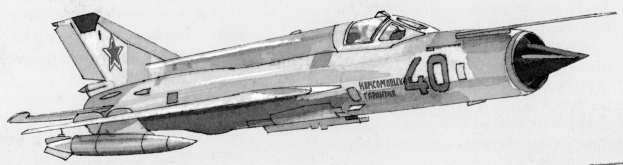

3. **MiG-21 Fishbed**
   (USSR 1956)
   Now one of the most widely used
   fighters

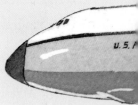